From Eden to Eternity Vol. II

by Abe C. Van Der Puy

Voice of Missions
Back to the Bible Broadcast

President
World Radio Missionary Fellowship

Back to the Bible

Lincoln, Nebraska 68501

80,000 printed to date—1981
(5-9991—80M—11)
ISBN 0-8474-0708-X

Unless otherwise identified, all Scripture quotations are
from the New American Standard Bible.

Cover photo by Bill Myers.

Printed in the United States of America

Contents

Chapter 1

Babel—Lessons From Disobedience

"Now the whole earth used the same language and the same words. And it came about as they journeyed east, that they found a plain in the land of Shinar and settled there. And they said to one another, 'Come, let us make bricks and burn them thoroughly.' And they used brick for stone, and they used tar for mortar. And they said, 'Come, let us build for ourselves a city, and a tower whose top will reach into heaven, and let us make for ourselves a name; lest we be scattered abroad over the face of the whole earth.' And the Lord came down to see the city and the tower which the sons of men had built. And the Lord said, 'Behold, they are one people, and they all have the same language. And this is what they began to do, and now nothing which they purpose to do will be impossible for them. Come, let Us go down and there confuse their language, that they may not understand one another's speech.' So the Lord scattered them abroad from there over the face of the whole earth; and they stopped building the city. Therefore its name was called Babel, because there the Lord confused the language of the whole earth; and from there the Lord scattered them abroad over the face of the whole earth" (Gen. 11:1-9).

God Confused Their Language

What a day it must have been when God confused the language of men. They had been speaking one common language. Then suddenly they found themselves trying to communicate in different languages. They experienced great surprises as they tried to continue the construction of the tower. The foreman gave instructions to the laborers. But they did not understand. His language had become different from theirs. The architect tried to explain the plans to the foreman. The foreman didn't comprehend. They were speaking completely different languages. Great confusion resulted. The building project had to be suspended.

Why Did God Do This?

Today we realize that the multiplicity of languages on the earth is a monument not to human ingenuity but to human sin. God confused the language of these people for two reasons.

They Wanted a Name for Themselves

First, in building the tower they wanted to make a name for themselves. By this desire they demonstrated that they were self-centered rather than God-centered. The person who lives for self is not only wasting his life, but he is also sinning against God.

A person all wrapped up in himself makes a very small package. If our purpose in life is to make a name for ourselves, then we miss the mark as far as God is concerned. This kind of living falls far

6

short of the noble purpose for which God has created us.

To counteract this human tendency, we need to look again at the example of the Lord Jesus. "For even the Son of Man did not come to be served, but to serve, and to give His life a ransom for many" (Mark 10:45). He came to do the will of His Father and to finish His work. He was not self-centered but God-centered. If we are God-centered, then one of our primary concerns will be to share the gospel with others. The greatest benefit we can give to others is to tell them the truth of God.

I am always inspired by men and women who do not keep thinking about themselves but who live to serve others. Recently we received great help from a retired person who assists in our mission. He did his work with great joy. We all profited from his enthusiasm. When we live for God and others, we produce good fruit in our lives. The people at the Tower of Babel made the big mistake of being self-centered rather than God-centered.

They Tried to Avoid Being Scattered

Second, they wanted to build the tower and the city to avoid being scattered abroad. They determined to preserve a unity which they didn't really have because sin divides. They sought oneness by some physical means or by organizational arrangement. In doing this they made several errors.

Because they didn't want to be scattered abroad, they directly disobeyed God. He had told them to be fruitful and to spread abroad upon the face of the earth (see Gen. 9:1). I suppose the people could have given many logical reasons for remaining

7

together. The fact of the matter was that God had told them to do the opposite.

So it often is with us. We can rationalize. We can present a good case. But the important question is "What does God say?" Frequently we inject our own reasoning into the matter of world evangelism. One day a smart young man asked the Duke of Wellington, "Sir, what do you think about the command of Jesus Christ to get the gospel to the whole earth?" The Duke replied, "As a soldier I have learned to obey orders. As I understand it, your orders are to go into all the world and preach the gospel to every creature." It is not an elective for us. We make a mistake if we rationalize another arrangement. Jesus has given the orders, and we should obey them.

At the Tower of Babel these people tried to accomplish something by building and organizing which, in reality, can take place only by right relationships with God. Man does the same thing today. He tries schemes, plans and conferences to bring unity in the world. But he will not succeed. Unity comes only as men and women are rightly related to the Lord. Here is the important personal application: Let's find the answer to our needs, problems and aspirations by genuinely trusting God, not by our own plotting apart from God.

The Prospect Before Us

The language confusion resulting from Babel presents us with the great challenge of reaching all people with God's message. The Holy Spirit promises to give us facility in doing God's work. Let us pray, give and minister in Jesus' name so

8

that every man and woman might hear the Good News in his own language. Then we can look forward to that great day when we will praise the Lord forever in heaven. We'll all speak one language again—the dialect of heaven. We'll do it perfectly because Jesus will present the Church to Himself "in all her glory, having no spot or wrinkle or any such thing" (Eph. 5:27).

Chapter 2

Abraham—Friend of God

"Now the Lord said to Abram, 'Go forth from your country, and from your relatives and from your father's house, to the land which I will show you; and I will make you a great nation, and I will bless you, and make your name great; and so you shall be a blessing; and I will bless those who bless you, and the one who curses you I will curse. And in you all the families of the earth shall be blessed.' So Abram went forth as the Lord had spoken to him; and Lot went with him. Now Abram was seventy-five years old when he departed from Haran. And Abram took Sarai his wife and Lot his nephew, and all their possessions which they had accumulated, and the persons which they had acquired in Haran, and they set out for the land of Canaan; thus they came to the land of Canaan. And Abram passed through the land as far as the site of Shechem, to the oak of Moreh. Now the Canaanite was then in the land. And the Lord appeared to Abram and said, 'To your descendants I will give this land.' So he built an altar there to the Lord who had appeared to him" (Gen. 12:1-7).

Abraham's Great Faith

The Bible calls Abraham the friend of God (James 2:23) and the father of believers (Rom.

4:16). Perhaps more than any other person in the Bible he gave us a marvelous demonstration of faith in God. Several passages in the New Testament emphasize Abraham's trust. For example, Romans 4:20,21 declares, "Yet, with respect to the promise of God, he did not waver in unbelief, but grew strong in faith, giving glory to God, and being fully assured that what He had promised, He was able also to perform." Also James 2:23 says, " 'And Abraham believed God, and it was reckoned to him as righteousness,' and he was called the friend of God."

Abraham's Obedience by Faith

God told Abraham to leave his country and relatives and go to a land which God would show him.

Leaving Everything Dear to Him

First, this involved leaving everything that was dear to him. It meant leaving a land of advanced civilization and of settled comfort. The difficulties of this step no doubt increased when Abraham's father died in Haran (see Gen. 11:32). Abraham went on without his father.

Going Without Knowing

Furthermore, the Bible tells us that in following God's plan, Abraham "went out, not knowing where he was going" (Heb. 11:8). God left many things unclear. More than that, the Lord promised to give the land to Abraham as an inheritance, but Abraham did not see the completion of that promise. Centuries later his descendants entered the land and took possession of it.

Meeting the Test

Right at the beginning Abraham's faith was tested. The land suffered famine (see Gen. 12:10). As Abraham looked at the brown landscape and the parched soil, he must have had many questions about God's plan. But even though he did go to Egypt for a short time, he ultimately believed God and did not lose confidence. This man of God did not merely believe that the bank was trustworthy; he made a deposit in it. He did not merely assent to the dependability of the bridge; he crossed it. He did not merely agree to the durability of the foundation; he built his life upon it.

John Oxenham wrote:

> Lord, give me faith to live from day to day,
> With tranquil heart to do my simple part,
> And with my hand in Thine just go Thy way;
> Lord, give me faith to trust, if not to know,
> With quiet mind in all things Thee to find,
> And, childlike, go where Thou wouldst have me go;
> Lord, give me faith to leave it all to Thee.
> The future is Thy gift; I would not lift
> The veil Thy love has flung 'twixt it and me.

God's Wonderful Promises for Faith

God told Abraham three things: "I will make you a great nation" (Gen. 12:2). "I will . . . make your name great" (v. 2). "In you all the families of the earth shall be blessed" (v. 3). You will remember that the people at Babel wanted to make a

12

name for themselves, and they failed. By contrast, the Lord said to this humble man of faith, "I will ... make your name great; and so you shall be a blessing" (v. 2). Isn't that what makes life truly successful?

When God called Abraham, he was not thinking only about him and his family. He intended to bless all nations through Abraham. Once more we have in view the missionary purpose of God. Our Lord has not changed that objective. As believers in Jesus Christ, we follow in the line of Abraham. To us God has also given precious promises. He blesses us that, in turn, all nations of the earth might receive God's blessing.

The friend of God "was looking for the city which has foundations, whose architect and builder is God" (Heb. 11:10). He looked far beyond the earthly country, Canaan, to a much better one. He was willing to live for a while in the earthly land as a pilgrim and a stranger, but he was looking beyond to the heavenly mansions. We need to ask the question, "Are our lives geared that way?" They should be.

Chapter 3

Abraham—Example of Goodness

"And the land could not sustain them while dwelling together; for their possessions were so great that they were not able to remain together. And there was strife between the herdsmen of Abram's livestock and the herdsmen of Lot's livestock. Now the Canaanite and the Perizzite were dwelling then in the land. Then Abram said to Lot, 'Please let there be no strife between you and me, nor between my herdsmen and your herdsmen, for we are brothers. Is not the whole land before you? Please separate from me: if to the left, then I will go to the right; or if to the right, then I will go to the left.' And Lot lifted up his eyes and saw all the valley of the Jordan, that it was well watered everywhere—this was before the Lord destroyed Sodom and Gomorrah—like the garden of the Lord, like the land of Egypt as you go to Zoar. So Lot chose for himself all the valley of the Jordan; and Lot journeyed eastward. Thus they separated from each other" (Gen. 13:6-11).

The Humility and Goodness of Faith

This is one of the most tremendous lessons in all of the Old Testament. Trouble began between the herdsmen of Abraham and those of Lot. It would have been easy for Abraham to have said, "Lot, we'll have to separate. You know that I'm the eldest. Besides, God has given me many promises concerning this land. First, I'll take what I need. Then you'll take what is left."

Amazingly, Abraham did just the opposite. He said, "Lot, we have a problem. But we can settle this very easily. You just take your choice of the pastures you need. I'll take what is left."

We Are Brothers

The true Christian does not insist on his rights. He always demonstrates magnanimity. Two important reasons are recommended for having this attitude. The first one Abraham expressed this way, "We are brothers" (Gen. 13:8). He recognized the close ties between them. He felt nothing was big enough to break that relationship. Nothing should come between Lot and him, for they were brothers.

That same principle holds true today. When we walk by faith, we take care to maintain Christian unity. We cherish the tie that binds us together as sisters and brothers. For this reason, Abraham gave the choice to Lot.

Confident in God's Promises

Second, Abraham believed the promises of God. It really didn't make any difference what land Lot chose to take. God would still carry out His promises. The person who trusts God does not need to struggle or fight. God will take care of working things out. When we have such convictions, then we can live in the humility and goodness of faith.

15

The Arrogance and Foolishness of Sight

The Bible says we should walk by faith and not by sight (see II Cor. 5:7). When Abraham treated Lot so kindly, Lot should have said, "Uncle Abraham, I appreciate your consideration. However, you should have first choice. I know that God has given you the prior claim on this land. I'll just fit into the picture as you wish." But Lot did not react that way. Unfortunately, many people do not respond to kindness as they should. They take advantage of the situation. Lot did that. He illustrated the arrogance and foolishness of living by sight.

Furthermore, in walking by sight, Lot made his decision with only material advantages in mind. The Bible adds the comment, "Now the men of Sodom were wicked exceedingly and sinners against the Lord" (Gen. 13:13). Today many people base their decisions solely upon material advantages and profits. Like Lot, they often lose everything in the end. Tragedy and sadness become the painful results.

By contrast Abraham received new promises from the Lord. Lot took advantage of Abraham, but he did not harm God's servant. Those who put God first always find Him working in their behalf.

Application to Our Work and Service

This story urges us to make our decisions on the basis of God's will. The will of God sets priorities for us in life.

Too many of us choose our priorities on the basis of getting. The one who follows God's will selects his priorities on the basis of giving. We can do no greater giving than telling men and women about God's gift of eternal life. In humility and faith we can serve as a blessing to others.

Every time we put God first, He comes to us and gives us new promises. They open up fresh vistas and new channels of ministry. There is no greater joy in life than to serve God and man.

Above everything else, it's a great privilege to reach out to people far from God and bring them to the Saviour. Many, very many, still need to hear the truth of God. Let's be sure we are an active part of God's team, participating in His plan to bless the world.

Chapter 4

Abraham's Courageous and Wise Actions

"And when Abram heard that his relative had been taken captive, he led out his trained men, born in his house, three hundred and eighteen, and went in pursuit as far as Dan. And he divided his forces against them by night, he and his servants, and defeated them, and pursued them as far as Hobah, which is north of Damascus. And he brought back all the goods, and also brought back his relative Lot with his possessions, and also the women, and the people. Then after his return from the defeat of Chedorlaomer and the kings who were with him, the king of Sodom went out to meet him at the valley of Shaveh (that is, the King's Valley). And Melchizedek king of Salem brought out bread and wine; now he was a priest of God Most High. And he blessed him and said, 'Blessed be Abram of God Most High, possessor of heaven and earth; and blessed be God Most High, who has delivered your enemies into your hand.' And he gave him a tenth of all. And the king of Sodom said to Abram, 'Give the people to me and take the goods for yourself.' And Abram said to the king of Sodom, 'I have sworn to the Lord God Most High, possessor of heaven and earth, that I will not take a thread or a sandal thong or anything that is yours, lest you should say, "I have made Abram

rich." I will take nothing except what the young
men have eaten, and the share of the men who
went with me, Aner, Eshcol, and Mamre; let them
take their share' " (Gen. 14:14-24).

The Greatness of Abraham

This passage of Scripture presents to us Abraham's courageous and wise actions. It lets us see
Abraham in an extraordinary role—as the com-
manding general of military forces, conducting a
campaign to rescue his nephew Lot who had been
captured in a battle involving nine kings.

This account gives us a good idea of the great-
ness of Abraham. He had 318 trained men, born in
his own household. Of course that would indicate
that many more persons formed the entire group
under Abraham's control.

Abraham was obviously a wealthy and important man. But although he was very wealthy, he
was beautifully detached from material things. He
considered them a trust from God. In this connection Abraham showed his magnanimity when he
came back from battle. The king of Sodom offered
to let him keep all the goods he had captured (see
Gen. 14:21). Abraham refused. He asked only for
reimbursement for the expenses he had encoun-
tered and nothing more. He did not have a desire to
accumulate more and more material things, especially at the expense of others.

Do we consider possessions a trust from God?
Some of us have a limited amount of material
things. They still come from God; we can still use
them wisely. Others of us have extensive holdings.
We are stewards of those possessions. God holds

us responsible for how we use them. They have been given to us by God to use for His glory and for the benefit of men and women.

The best investment that we can make of material things is to use them to speed the gospel of Jesus Christ to the ends of the earth. I thank God for the men and women who diligently use what God has given them to support missions and to send out missionaries because they desire to get the gospel to the lost. We need to decide. We can either spend things on ourselves, lavishly and unwisely, or we can carefully spend our resources for God's work and use them for the extension of the gospel.

Abraham's Willingness to Accept God's Arrangements

In this Scripture passage we see another side of Abraham's personality and character. It shows us how willing he was to conform to God's arrangements. After Abraham's victory, Melchizedek went out to meet him (see Gen. 14:18-20). Melchizedek was a priest of the most high God. He brought refreshment to the tired warriors. Then two things happened: He blessed Abraham in the name of the Lord, and Abraham paid tithes to Melchizedek.

Hebrews 7 refers to this incident: "For this Melchizedek, king of Salem, priest of the Most High God, who met Abraham as he was returning from the slaughter of the kings and blessed him, to whom also Abraham apportioned a tenth part of all the spoils, was first of all, by the translation of his name, king of righteousness, and then also king of Salem, which is king of peace" (vv. 1,2).

Many other men, flushed with victory and owning many possessions, might not have been ready to recognize the superiority of Melchizedek's position. Here again Abraham showed his true colors, his faith in God and his desire to obey the Lord in every way. Abraham was willing to follow God's commands, to do God's will and to carry out God's purpose. Abraham recognized Melchizedek as a priest of God, was blessed by him and paid tithes to him.

You and I need to be concerned about doing God's will today. In the midst of achievements and honors we can easily be tempted to become proud, to forget God and to fail in keeping His commandments. The Scriptures set forth the will of God. It's wonderful to be obedient to Him. We should be especially concerned about obeying God in the matter of sharing the gospel with others, in carrying the good news of salvation to the ends of the earth. God wishes to work powerfully in our lives to make us good witnesses. Let's be like Abraham in this regard—very much aware of the promises and commands of God and concerned about carrying them out. Then God will be able to say to us also, "I will bless you and make you a blessing." There is no greater wealth than to be blessed by God and, in turn, to serve as a blessing to others.

Chapter 5

God Confirms His Promises

"After these things the word of the Lord came to Abram in a vision, saying, 'Do not fear, Abram, I am a shield to you; your reward shall be very great.' And Abram said, 'O Lord God, what wilt Thou give me, since I am childless, and the heir of my house is Eliezer of Damascus?' And Abram said, 'Since Thou hast given no offspring to me, one born in my house is my heir.' Then behold, the word of the Lord came to him, saying, 'This man will not be your heir; but one who shall come forth from your own body, he shall be your heir.' And He took him outside and said, 'Now look toward the heavens, and count the stars, if you are able to count them.' And He said to him, 'So shall your descendants be.' Then he believed in the Lord; and He reckoned it to him as righteousness. . . . Now when the sun was going down, a deep sleep fell upon Abram; and behold, terror and great darkness fell upon him. And God said to Abram, 'Know for certain that your descendants will be strangers in a land that is not theirs, where they will be enslaved and oppressed four hundred years. But I will also judge the nation whom they will serve; and afterward they will come out with many possessions. And as for you, you shall go to your fathers in peace; you shall be buried at a good old age' " (Gen. 15:1-6, 12-15).

Abraham States His Problem

The renewal of God's promises to Abraham came at a very appropriate time. Abraham had just won a great victory. However, he also found himself in a difficult position. God had promised to make of him a great nation, but he had no heirs. That made everything seem terribly contradictory.

Abraham said, "Lord God, what wilt Thou give me, since I am childless?" (Gen. 15:2). The situation looked hopeless, impossible, unbelievable. Abraham was concerned; yet in spite of this, the sacred record indicates he continued to believe God.

Abraham faced problems. He expressed them freely to the Lord. We should do the same. Do you have concerns? Do you have questions? Is some problem preoccupying your mind? Perhaps you do not understand some things—they bother you. I suggest you lay these matters openly and frankly before God. Tell Him that you love Him and that you believe in Him but that some things disturb you. Ask for the guidance and illumination of the Holy Spirit. It may be that, just as in the case of Abraham, God is preparing you through a great problem to receive great things from Him.

God Confirms His Promises

"Abram, I am a shield to you; your reward shall be very great" (Gen. 15:1). God promised protection. At the same time He taught where our deepest joy must be. God is our greatest reward. The Lord Himself is more important than all His gifts. The most abiding joys are in God Himself.

"Now look toward the heavens, and count the stars, if you are able to count them. . . . So shall your descendants be" (v. 5). Abraham's apparently impossible situation did not change the promise of God. God works in impossible circumstances. The sooner we learn that the better.

This particular promise of God concerned the descendants of Abraham. They would be as many as the stars of the sky and the grains of sand on the seashore. To his credit, Abraham firmly believed God.

The Lord offers to give us descendants too—spiritual sons and daughters who will trust in Him as we share our faith with them. It was God's purpose for Abraham to have many descendants; it is also God's purpose for His Son, the Lord Jesus, to have many descendants, or followers. Therefore, Jesus commanded us, "Go into all the world and preach the gospel to all creation" (Mark 16:15).

God Counts It for Righteousness

Abraham could not see the realization of the promises, but he was willing to accept God's word and to act upon it. He committed himself entirely to the Lord, putting his life in God's hands. God counted it to him for righteousness. By trusting God we receive His resources and provisions—including the provision of salvation in His Son, Jesus Christ.

This is the exchanged life—not my weakness but God's strength, not my sin but God's righteousness, not my failures but God's triumphs. How tremendous this is—the life of God works through us.

24

God Seeks to Help Us

What kind of faith do we have in the Lord? Do we believe Him for daily needs? For the blessing we want to be? It also takes trust in God's guidance to make us a part of His world program. He will use us in the right way, in the right place, with the right power. Then we can contribute to the outreach of the gospel of our Lord Jesus Christ. The same God who helped Abraham so wonderfully will also help us to serve Him well.

Amy Carmichael expressed this desire to be used by God in her book *Toward Jerusalem:*

Make us Thy labourers,
Let us not dream of ever looking back,
Let not our knees be feeble, hands be slack,
O make us strong to labour, strong to bear,
From the rising of the morning till the stars appear.

Make us Thy warriors,
On whom Thou canst depend to stand the brunt
Of any perilous charge on any front,
Give to us skill to handle sword and spear,
From the rising of the morning till the stars appear.

Not far from us, those stars,
Unseen as angels and yet looking through
The quiet air, the day's transparent blue.
What shall we know, and feel, and see, and hear
When the sunset colours kindle and the stars appear?

Chapter 6

Failure and Faithfulness

"Now Sarai, Abram's wife had borne him no children, and she had an Egyptian maid whose name was Hagar. So Sarai said to Abram, 'Now behold, the Lord has prevented me from bearing children. Please go in to my maid; perhaps I shall obtain children through her.' And Abram listened to the voice of Sarai. And after Abram had lived ten years in the land of Canaan, Abram's wife Sarai took Hagar the Egyptian, her maid, and gave her to her husband Abram as his wife. And he went in to Hagar, and she conceived; and when she saw that she had conceived, her mistress was despised in her sight. And Sarai said to Abram, 'May the wrong done me be upon you. I gave my maid into your arms; but when she saw that she had conceived, I was despised in her sight. May the Lord judge between you and me.' But Abram said to Sarai, 'Behold, your maid is in your power; do to her what is good in your sight.' So Sarai treated her harshly, and she fled from her presence. . . . So Hagar bore Abram a son; and Abram called the name of his son, whom Hagar bore, Ishmael. And Abram was eighty-six years old when Hagar bore Ishmael to him" (Gen. 16:1-6, 15,16).

Sad Results of Not Waiting for God

When the promised heir did not arrive, Sarah encouraged Abraham to take Hagar for his wife, which he did. In doing that, both Sarah and Abraham sinned. Immediately, trouble began. Hagar began to feel superior to Sarah. Conflict resulted. Sarah said to Abraham, "The wrong done to me is your fault" (see Gen. 16:5).

This story illustrates what always happens. If we forsake the ways of the Lord, if we do not trust Him, trouble always results. This spiritual law is just as certain as the fact that two plus two equals four. Some of us are experiencing this right now. We did not listen to God, we did not follow His way, and now we are in trouble. The results of disobedience surround us and follow us. It's much better to do the will of God.

Some kinds of disobedience are more obvious than others. A thief obviously breaks the law, and punishment often comes quickly. We all recognize that a bad temper dishonors God. But we can also disobey in other ways that are not so obvious to other people. I think, for example, of God's call to all believers to be an active part of His team, carrying the message of light to those who do not know Jesus Christ. If we do not obey God in this matter, we can never have a fully prosperous spiritual life. Let's do God's will and follow Him.

The Mercy of God to Hagar

Hagar fled. She found herself alone by a spring of water in the wilderness. The angel of the Lord found her. "She called the name of the Lord that

27

spake unto her, Thou God seest me" (Gen. 16:13, KJV). This reminds us that the Lord is everywhere. No matter where we go, He is there. The psalmist said, "Thou dost know when I sit down and when I rise up; Thou dost understand my thought from afar. Thou dost scrutinize my path and my lying down, and art intimately acquainted with all my ways" (Ps. 139:2,3).

Everyone is known to God and is important to Him. Some might have said of Hagar, "Let her go; no one will miss her. It's better that she stays away or disappears completely." Not so with God. No matter how insignificant a person may appear to be, God has a wonderful purpose for him.

Right now you may feel all alone; you may feel insignificant. You may have no purpose in life. My dear friend, God sees you, loves you and wants to help you. He desires you to have a wonderfully useful life. You are important to Him. Trust Him for that. Let God take control of your life. He will make it valuable. Your life will shine with the glory and power of God.

The truth that everyone is important to God constitutes a great cornerstone for world evangelism. The large numbers of people whom you and I do not know are important to God. The ones who live at the edge of civilization, who don't have any idea of what the rest of the world is like, are known and loved by God.

God's Faithfulness Continues

Genesis 16 also teaches us that God's faithfulness continues in spite of our failures. God could have said to Sarah and Abraham, "You spoiled it

28

all. You have not kept your side of the bargain, so neither will I." Thank God, He did not do that. He kept His promises. He did this in spite of the misdemeanor of Sarah and Abraham. Our failures, too, are many. It's wonderful to know that God does not react to our unfaithfulness with an equal measure of unfaithfulness. We may fail, but He keeps His promises (see II Tim. 2:13).

All of this reminds us again that we are defective instruments, or what the Bible calls "earthen vessels" (II Cor. 4:7). By ourselves and in ourselves we are not worth much. But we mean a great deal to God and are important in relationship to Him. A vessel, or container, which is not of great value in itself can become valuable by reason of what it contains. You and I as believers possess the presence, power and glory of God. When His life shines through us, it brings glory to God.

We are of value to God. What we do is important to Him. This truth takes on special meaning as we do God's will by taking the gospel to lost men and women. Such service puts meaning, dignity and sparkle into life. The glory of God surrounds and indwells us. Let us take courage in that fact and move forward.

Chapter 7

The Sealing of God's Covenant

"Now when Abram was ninety-nine years old, the Lord appeared to Abram and said to him, 'I am God Almighty; walk before Me, and be blameless. And I will establish My covenant between Me and you, and I will multiply you exceedingly.' And Abram fell on his face, and God talked with him, saying, 'As for Me, behold, My covenant is with you, and you shall be the father of a multitude of nations. No longer shall your name be called Abram, but your name shall be Abraham; for I will make you the father of a multitude of nations. And I will make you exceedingly fruitful, and I will make nations of you, and kings shall come forth from you.' . . . 'This is My covenant, which you shall keep, between Me and you and your descendants after you: every male among you shall be circumcised. And you shall be circumcised in the flesh of your foreskin; and it shall be the sign of the covenant between Me and you. And every male among you who is eight days old shall be circumcised throughout your generations, a servant who is born in the house or who is bought with money from any foreigner, who is not of your descendants. A servant who is born in your house or who is bought with your money shall surely be circumcised; thus shall My covenant be in your flesh for an everlasting covenant. But an uncircumcised male who is not circumcised in the flesh of his foreskin, that person shall be cut off from his people; he has broken My covenant.' Then God said to Abraham, 'As for Sarai your wife, you shall not call her name Sarai, but Sarah shall be her name. And I will bless her, and indeed I will give you a son by her. Then I will bless her, and she shall be a mother of nations; kings of peoples shall come from her' " (Gen. 17:1-6,10-16).

Once again in this chapter God repeated His promises to Abraham. A man of lesser faith would have felt that God was mocking him. But Abraham did not. We see indications in this story that his heart was almost stretched to the breaking point. He experienced great confusion. God was giving him all these promises, yet the fact remained that he had no heir. He was still childless. How beautiful then to see Abraham submitting to the promises and commands of the Lord. He could not understand it all, but he did trust. The Bible says that Abraham fell on his face before God. In that act he confirmed his continuing worship of the Lord and his strong faith in his God.

God gave two signs, or seals, of the covenant He had made with Abraham.

The Changing of Sarah's and Abraham's Names

First, the Lord changed the names of Sarah and Abraham. Instead of Sarai and Abram, they became Sarah and Abraham. "Abraham" means "father of a multitude." "Sarah" means "princess." It's significant that God made this name change before Isaac was born. This required faith on Abraham's and Sarah's part. In fact, this demanded faith in its purest form. They still had no tangible evidence that they would have descendants, yet God described Abraham as the father of a multitude and Sarah as a princess with a view to her reign over many descendants.

It's a beautiful thing to trust God so much that we believe before we have tangible signs of the fulfillment of His promises. "Faith is the assurance of things hoped for, the conviction of things not seen" (Heb. 11:1). Marcus Dods said, "Faith is not a blind and careless assent to matters of indifference, faith is not a state of mental suspense with a hope that things will turn out as the Bible says. Faith is the firm persuasion that these things are so" (*The Expositor's Bible,* Vol. 1, p. 47). May God help us to have that kind of trust today.

The Rite of Circumcision

Then God gave Abraham and his people the sign of circumcision. Every male child among them who was at least eight days old was required to be circumcised. Though an external ceremony, it had deep spiritual importance. It is described very well in Colossians 2:11: "And in Him [Christ] you were also circumcised with a circumcision made without hands, in the removal of the body of the flesh by the circumcision of Christ." This really tells us that we have no acceptance with God unless we are cleansed from sin by the blood of Christ.

The sign of circumcision spoke eloquently about the cutting away of sinful desires and actions. It foreshadowed the work of Jesus Christ as it sealed the covenant God made with Abraham. Abraham accepted God's directions. He believed and obeyed

God. All the men of his household were circumcised—a sign of God's blessing, the completion of which Abraham had not yet seen.

The Call to Us

The call to us from this chapter is "Have faith in God." Exercise faith for daily needs, faith for God to empower us so we can serve Him, faith that God will keep His promises in connection with world evangelization.

When Jesus gave the command to go with the gospel to everyone everywhere, He surrounded it with two wonderful promises: "All authority has been given to Me in heaven and on earth" (Matt. 28:18) and "Lo, I am with you always, even to the end of the age" (v. 20). Often carrying out Jesus' command seems to be an impossibility—just as Abraham's situation appeared to be impossible. But the Lord's promises surround and support His commands. Like Abraham, you and I can accept the promises and stand on them with confidence. Have faith in God. He will reward those who diligently seek Him.

Augustine prayed, "Give what you command, and command what you will."

> Faith, mighty faith, the promise sees,
> And looks to God alone;
> Laughs at impossibilities,
> And cries it shall be done;
> And cries it shall, it shall be done,
> And cries it shall, it shall be done;
> Laughs at impossibilities,
> And cries it shall be done.

Chapter 8

God Talks With Abraham

"Now the Lord appeared to him by the oaks of Mamre, while he was sitting at the tent door in the heat of the day. And when he lifted up his eyes and looked, behold, three men were standing opposite him; and when he saw them, he ran from the tent door to meet them, and bowed himself to the earth, and said, 'My lord, if now I have found favor in your sight, please do not pass your servant by. Please let a little water be brought and wash your feet, and rest yourselves under the tree; and I will bring a piece of bread, that you may refresh yourselves; after that you may go on, since you have visited your servant.' And they said, 'So do, as you have said.' So Abraham hurried into the tent to Sarah, and said, 'Quickly, prepare three measures of fine flour, knead it, and make bread cakes.' Abraham also ran to the herd, and took a tender and choice calf, and gave it to the servant; and he hurried to prepare it. And he took curds and milk and the calf which he had prepared, and placed it before them; and he was standing by them under the tree as they ate. . . . Then the men rose up from there, and looked down toward Sodom; and Abraham was walking with them to send them off. And the Lord said, 'Shall I hide from Abraham what I am about to do, since Abraham will surely become a great and mighty nation, and in him all the nations of the earth will be blessed? For I have chosen him, in order that he may command his children and his household after him to keep the way of the Lord by doing righteousness and justice; in order that the Lord may bring upon Abraham what He has spoken about him.' And the Lord said, 'The outcry of Sodom and Gomorrah is indeed great, and their sin is exceedingly grave' " (Gen. 18:1-8,16-20).

We have seen that Abraham lived in wonderful communion with God. He was called "the friend of God" (James 2:23). Genesis 18 illustrates this fact in a special way.

The Hospitality of Abraham

The Bible tells us that three men stood before Abraham. He didn't know them, yet he immediately offered them the finest hospitality. He put everything he had at their disposal. By reading the story carefully we discover that the visitors were angels, or heavenly messengers. The Bible says, "The Lord appeared to him by the oaks of Mamre" (Gen. 18:1). These angels represented the Lord.

Remember, the Bible says in Hebrews 13:2, "Do not neglect to show hospitality to strangers, for by this some have entertained angels without knowing it." In Matthew 25:35 Jesus declared, "I was a stranger, and you invited Me in." And a few verses later He said, "Truly I say to you, to the extent that you did it to one of these brothers of Mine, even the least of them, you did it to Me" (v. 40). Christian hospitality to strangers is clearly and emphatically taught in the Word of God.

We need to ask the questions, "How much of this

kind of hospitality do we show these days? Do we reach out to help total strangers in Christian love if we can?" In the far corners of the earth, one of the finest things missionaries do is to exercise the gift of hospitality. Their homes have become havens. People are welcomed and loved there. When that happens, the door also opens widely to present the gospel of our Lord Jesus Christ. If you are looking for Christian witnessing opportunities, then show hospitality.

We ought to exercise hospitality primarily because God tells us to do it but also because such service becomes a great channel for sharing the truth of God.

God Reveals His Secrets to Abraham

God said, "Shall I hide from Abraham that thing which I do?" (Gen. 18:17, KJV). In other words, God desired to take Abraham into His confidence. This reminds us immediately of Psalm 25:14: "The secret of the Lord is for those who fear Him." Friendship with God belongs to those who reverence Him. With such people alone He shares His secrets. God does not have favorites, but He does have those who enjoy intimate friendship with Him. That's life's greatest privilege—to live in communion with God.

Real life comes through fellowship with God. Many people wonder why things aren't clear to them. The purposes of God seem strange. I think the basic reason this happens is that we do not know God. When we know Him through intimate communion and when we follow God's directions, then, like Abraham, we become friends of God and He reveals His secrets to us.

36

Abraham Intercedes for Sodom

God revealed to Abraham that he planned to destroy Sodom and Gomorrah. Abraham pleaded for Sodom. He said, "If there are 50 righteous people, will You save it? If there are 45? If there are 40? If there are 30? If there are 20? If there are 10?" (see Gen. 18:23-32). God replied, "I will save the city if I can find ten righteous people there" (see v. 32).

This incident reveals both the boldness and the humility of prevailing prayer. We must pray humbly, of course, but God wants us to lay our hearts bare before Him and to boldly ask of Him. I trust that prayer is a genuine, vital force in our lives.

Some years ago I heard a person say, "We don't need anything else right now but the power of God, and that can't be sent by anyone except via the throne of God." You and I desire power in life—power with God and power with men—all for the glory of God. That comes through earnest prayer before God. God listened to Abraham's prayer and would have honored it if He had found ten righteous people. You and I can have that same kind of power in prayer.

This matter of prayer has a vital connection with the big task of getting the gospel to those who have never heard it. The Lord calls us to go to every creature with His message (see Mark 16:15). Since that is so, I'm sure it pleases God when we come to Him, praying for those who still need to hear the gospel of Christ.

It's good to have a prayer list for the cities, provinces and tribes that are still without the gospel. Plead for their salvation. Pray with faith and trust. That's an important exercise. God will hear and answer prayer. We've seen God do it over and over again. It can happen many times more. So trust God as Abraham did. You will be blessed, and others will be blessed too.

Chapter 9

The Destruction of Sodom

"And when morning dawned, the angels urged Lot, saying, 'Up, take your wife and your two daughters, who are here, lest you be swept away in the punishment of the city.' But he hesitated. So the men seized his hand and the hand of his wife and the hands of his daughters, for the compassion of the Lord was upon him; and they brought him out, and put him outside the city. And it came about when they had brought them outside, that one said, 'Escape for your life! Do not look behind you, and do not stay anywhere in the valley; escape to the mountains, lest you be swept away.' But Lot said to them, 'Oh no, my lords! Now behold, your servant has found favor in your sight, and you have magnified your lovingkindness, which you have shown me by saving my life; but I cannot escape to the mountains, lest the disaster overtake me and I die; now behold, this town is near enough to flee to, and it is small. Please, let me escape there (is it not small?) that my life may be saved.' And he said to him, 'Behold, I grant you this request also, not to overthrow the town of which you have spoken. Hurry, escape there, for I cannot do anything until you arrive there.' Therefore the name of the town was called Zoar. The sun had risen over the earth when Lot came to Zoar. Then the Lord rained on Sodom and Gomorrah brimstone and fire from the Lord out of heaven, and He overthrew those cities, and all the valley, and all the inhabitants of the cities, and what grew on the ground. But his wife, from behind him, looked back; and she became a pillar of salt" (Gen. 19:15-26).

The Judgment of God

God rained brimstone and fire out of heaven on Sodom and Gomorrah. He overthrew those cities "and what grew on the ground" (Gen. 19:25). Desolation prevailed.

Genesis 6—9 contains the account of the flood. God promised to never again destroy all the inhabitants of the earth with a flood (9:8-17). However, a small section of humanity and one part of the earth—Sodom and Gomorrah—was destroyed by fire and brimstone because their wickedness was very great. The story reminds us of the verse which says, "Do not be deceived, God is not mocked; for whatever a man sows, this he will also reap" (Gal. 6:7). As we think about this, we certainly should have a reverent fear of God.

Second Peter informs us that a time is coming when the world will be destroyed and the elements will melt with a fervent heat: "But the day of the Lord will come like a thief, in which the heavens will pass away with a roar and the elements will be destroyed with intense heat, and the earth and its works will be burned up. Since all these things are to be destroyed in this way, what sort of people ought you to be in holy conduct and godliness, looking for and hastening the coming of the day of God, on account of which the heavens will be destroyed by burning, and the elements will melt with intense heat! But according to His promise we are looking for new heavens and a new earth, in which righteousness dwells. Therefore, beloved, since you look for these things, be diligent to be found by Him in peace, spotless and blameless" (3:10-14).

In view of what is going to happen, we should be holy and godly. When great disasters or upheavals occur in nature, let us reflect on God's power. We should remember that He will destroy this old world and that He will bring into being new heavens and a new earth.

The Deliverance of Lot

Lot and his family were saved. Even though he had sinned and had not put God first, he was called "righteous Lot" (II Pet. 2:7). Of course he committed great sin by constantly living with evil and not doing anything about it. He evidently was concerned about the evil, but he did not take the active role he should have in combating it, for the Bible says that he "felt his righteous soul tormented day after day with their lawless deeds" (v. 8).

Many people are that way. Evil bothers them, yet for any number of reasons they do not wish to separate from it. It is commendable not to be involved in evil, but it is much better to actively pursue holiness and service for God.

Lot's wife looked back. She slowed down. It was with reluctance that she left the city. God's messengers had told them not to look back. She disobeyed and was immediately changed into a pillar of salt. Someone will say, "She certainly was foolish. She should have run for her life." But

41

wait a minute. Don't some of us do the very same thing that Lot's wife did? The end of life rushes upon us very swiftly, yet many of us have not made adequate preparation. We have not gotten our priorities straight. We are more concerned about the things of the world than about the things of God.

The other day a few of us were having a meal in a restaurant. A friend eating with us pointed out a young man at another table. That young man had apparently started out well in the Christian life but now was walking far from God because certain worldly things had become very attractive to him. He forgot God.

Marcus Dods said this in his commentary on Genesis 19: "Lot's wife by her death proclaims that if we crave to make the best of both worlds, we shall probably lose both. . . . She is not the only woman whose heart is so fixedly set upon her household possessions that she cannot listen to the angel-voices that would guide her. . . . For radically it was her divided mind which was her ruin. . . . What else is it ruins half the people who suppose themselves well on the way of life? The world is in their heart; they cannot pursue with undivided mind the promptings of a better wisdom. Their heart is with their treasure, and their treasure is really not in spiritual excellence, not in purity of character, not in the keen bracing air of the silent mountains where God is known, but in the comforts and gains of the luxurious plain behind" (*The Expositor's Bible*, Vol. 1, p. 53).

The call comes to us to have our priorities in order. The worship and the service of God are indispensable. They must be at the center of our lives. Then everything else can fit beautifully around that center. Furthermore, one of the Bible's great priorities is gospel outreach—getting the truth of Jesus Christ to those who have not heard about Him. When we hear many voices calling to us, let's be certain we listen to God's command to carry the message of life to other people in Jesus' name.

Chapter 10

Abraham's Sin

"Now Abraham journeyed from there toward the land of the Negev, and settled between Kadesh and Shur; then he sojourned in Gerar. And Abraham said of Sarah his wife, 'She is my sister.' So Abimelech king of Gerar sent and took Sarah. But God came to Abimelech in a dream of the night, and said to him, 'Behold, you are a dead man because of the woman whom you have taken, for she is married.' Now Abimelech had not come near her; and he said, 'Lord, wilt Thou slay a nation, even though blameless? Did he not himself say to me, "She is my sister"? And she herself said, "He is my brother." In the integrity of my heart and the innocence of my hands I have done this.' Then God said to him in the dream, 'Yes, I know that in the integrity of your heart you have done this, and I also kept you from sinning against Me; therefore I did not let you touch her. Now therefore restore the man's wife, for he is a prophet, and he will pray for you, and you will live. But if you do not restore her, know that you shall surely die, you and all who are yours.' So Abimelech arose early in the morning and called all his servants and told all these things in their hearing; and the men were greatly frightened. Then Abimelech called Abraham and said to him, 'What have you done to us? And how have I sinned against you, that you have brought on me and on my kingdom a great sin?

You have done to me things that ought not to be done' " (Gen. 20:1-9).

The Bible—A Faithful Record

Earlier in the Book of Genesis, we read how Noah, a godly, righteous man, fell into drunkenness in a moment of weakness (see 9:20-29). He brought disgrace upon himself and his family. In Genesis 20 we find something similar. Abraham—friend of God, father of believers—stooped to an act unworthy of him, of his position, of his spiritual maturity and of the promises of God to him.

When we read these accounts about men such as Noah and Abraham, we see that the Bible presents a faithful and accurate record. Even when we are dealing with heroes of the faith, the Bible truly reveals their points of weakness and difficulty. The Scriptures do this with restraint and good taste, yet the Word of God shows us that every human being—including believers—experiences failure and sin.

The Most Outstanding Is Still Imperfect

The most outstanding Christian among us is still imperfect. He must depend upon God every moment for strength and wisdom to defeat Satan. This truth should make us sober and alert.

It may be that one of us has become cocky in his spiritual life. You think you have it made and have everything under control. God says, "Let him who thinks he stands take heed lest he fall" (I Cor. 10:12). Today especially, with so much temptation and so many sinful attractions surrounding us, many who seemed very strong spiritually have fallen terribly. We, too, can fall unless we humbly trust in the power of God.

The reverse is also true. The weakest person among us who understands the necessity of drawing upon God's resources can become the strongest. When we depend upon God that way, He can make us useful and fruitful in the Christian life. We will never be able to fill God's place for us unless we have a sober understanding of our own limitations and weaknesses and unless we realize, at the same time, that through the Lord we can be strong, powerful and victorious.

The Sin of Lying

What was Abraham's sin? He lied about his relationship to Sarah. He told Abimelech, "She is my sister" (Gen. 20:2). After Abimelech had taken Sarah, God appeared to him in a dream and said to him, "Behold, you are a dead man because of the woman whom you have taken, for she is married" (v. 3). Those words certainly impress us with the importance and honor God gives to the marriage relationship. Many people today are ignoring that, but they do it to their own detriment. We cannot go against the commandments of God without suffering for it.

Just as so many other incidents in the Bible do, this story teaches the sinfulness of lying. Abraham thought he had a good reason for what he did. He feared being killed so that others could take his wife. And in a sense, Sarah was his sister—a half sister. This was a half-truth, but half-truths are not acceptable.

46

Jesus said, "I am the way, and the truth, and the life" (John 14:6). If we follow Him, then we must also be followers of truth. The Devil, on the other hand, is the "father of lies" (8:44). We live in an age of deceit—deceit in advertising, deceit in statements made by our leaders, deceit on every hand. Therefore, the followers of Jesus Christ should especially distinguish themselves by transparent honesty, by telling the truth no matter what it costs. Telling the truth and living honestly constitute a great testimony to people around us.

Lying often appears to be easier than telling the truth. It appears to get us out of difficulties. The problem with lying is that it has to continue. If a person lies, he always has to remember what he said in order to carry on the deceit. It's much better to tell the truth at all times.

In many cases when we sin, we not only get ourselves into trouble, but we also get others involved. In this situation, Abimelech and his whole household were affected by Abraham's sin. In this contradictory situation, a man who was not a believer exhorted and warned Abraham. The Bible tells us that we do not live to ourselves. Our actions either help or hinder others, they either inspire or disillusion, they either bless or curse.

Lying Results From Lack of Trust

What Abraham did stemmed from lack of trust in God. He took matters into his own hands. He felt he could handle them better than God could. That is always a mistake. We need to be sure that in all areas of life—the pleasant as well as the difficult ones—we will trust God and His principles, no matter what the cost.

Our lives influence others for either good or bad. That concerns people near at hand and far away. We need to be praying regularly, "O God, use my life to bless and challenge other people—not only my neighbors but also those far away who have never heard the gospel. Lord, by my praying, giving and going, let me be part of the team that is carrying on Your work so that those who are not Christians might today become Christians, that they might hear the truth of God and follow the way of life. Amen."

the son of the maid shall not be an heir…
…use of his descendant." (Gen. 21:1.)

Isaac is born

Isaac…
Enmity…
…use of Ishmael

Chapter 11

The Birth of Isaac, Trouble With Ishmael

"Then the Lord took note of Sarah as He had said, and the Lord did for Sarah as He had promised. So Sarah conceived and bore a son to Abraham in his old age, at the appointed time of which God had spoken to him. And Abraham called the name of his son who was born to him, whom Sarah bore to him, Isaac. Then Abraham circumcised his son Isaac when he was eight days old, as God had commanded him. Now Abraham was one hundred years old when his son Isaac was born to him. And Sarah said, 'God has made laughter for me; everyone who hears will laugh with me.' And she said, 'Who would have said to Abraham that Sarah would nurse children? Yet I have borne him a son in his old age.' And the child grew and was weaned, and Abraham made a great feast on the day that Isaac was weaned. Now Sarah saw the son of Hagar the Egyptian, whom she had borne to Abraham, mocking. Therefore, she said to Abraham, 'Drive out this maid and her son, for the son of this maid shall not be an heir with my son Isaac.' And the matter distressed Abraham greatly because of his son. But God said to Abraham, 'Do not be distressed because of the lad and your maid; whatever Sarah tells you, listen to her, for through Isaac your descendants shall be named. And of

49

the son of the maid I will make a nation also, because he is your descendant' " (Gen. 21:1-13).

Isaac Is Born

Isaac's birth must have been cause for great rejoicing in the household of Abraham.

A Time of Rejoicing

At last an heir was born according to the promise of God. His name was Isaac, which means, "he laughs." Everything spoke of festivity and rejoicing. The promise of God was fulfilled. Just as God kept His promise to Sarah and Abraham, He will do so today. We can find nothing more certain than the promises of God. Trust Him. Rest in Him. You will experience the genuine laughter which comes as you see God carrying out His promises.

We can experience nothing greater in life than to trust God and to see His promises carried out. When that happens, then we have deep joy in our hearts. No joy can compare to that which God's children have when they see His faithfulness. I'm reminded of the new believer who said in his testimony that he was happier as a believer, even in his unhappy moments, than he had ever been as an unbeliever, even in his happiest moments. Isaac—"he laughs." This was a time of rejoicing. Those who trust God have the joy of God.

A Set Time

The Bible says that the birth of Isaac occurred at God's appointed time (see Gen. 21:2). Sarah gave birth according to God's timetable. It was the right time, the set time, the time God had planned. God was not late. I hope you have great confidence in God's timing.

This makes us think about the coming of our Saviour, the Lord Jesus Christ. He came in "the fulness of the time" (Gal. 4:4). I suppose that if we had been living at the time Jesus came, we would not have thought that the circumstances were exactly right for the coming of the Messiah. But now we can see that He came at the right point in history. He arrived when His ministry and the work of the apostolic church had the greatest effect.

God always acts on time. If there are some things we do not understand, let us have patience and trust. Right now events in the world look very discouraging. The upheaval, chaos, anarchy and violence disturb us. But you and I need to believe that God can use us in a timely, strategic way in the midst of these contrary events. When people's hearts are failing them for fear, when the world doesn't know how to handle its problems, that's the best time to interject the message of the gospel of Christ.

The Conflict Between Isaac and Ishmael

The joy of Abraham's household was tempered by the conflict between Isaac and Ishmael. Soon serious trouble began. Ishmael began to mock Isaac. The Epistle to the Galatians tells us that this is a type of the conflict between the child of the promise and the child who is not of the promise, between grace and Law, between Spirit and flesh.

51

They have nothing in common. Galatians exhorts us to cast out the child of the bondwoman; that is, the works of the Law and the spirit of the slave (Gal. 4:30). We should rather enjoy liberty as the children of God. That liberty comes by receiving the salvation provided by Jesus Christ and becoming part of the family of God.

The entire Epistle to the Galatians urges us to enter fully and wholly into God's wonderful plan. What is this plan? God's Word makes it plain that we are sinners in need of salvation. But Jesus died for sinners. When we trust Him as Saviour, we have forgiveness of sins, receive eternal life and become sons of God. Consequently, we live by God's power.

In this relationship we do not advance by keeping regulations and ceremonial law. We progress by the dynamic life of God in us. We walk by the Holy Spirit to do the will of God and to carry out the service of God. Then we live to bless others. Then God says to us, "What you have learned you can now pass on to others. Do this not only with those who are near you but also with the tribes, peoples and nations who are far away, who have not heard the gospel of Jesus Christ." Each one of us needs to say, "Lord, help me to fit into Your plan for the evangelization of the world. I want to respond to Your call and purpose."

Chapter 12

The Obedience of Faith

"Now it came about after these things, that God tested Abraham, and said to him, 'Abraham!' And he said, 'Here I am.' And He said, 'Take now your son, your only son, whom you love, Isaac, and go to the land of Moriah; and offer him there as a burnt offering on one of the mountains of which I will tell you.' So Abraham rose early in the morning and saddled his donkey, and took two of his young men with him and Isaac his son; and he split wood for the burnt offering, and arose and went to the place of which God had told him. On the third day Abraham raised his eyes and saw the place from a distance. And Abraham said to his young men, 'Stay here with the donkey, and I and the lad will go yonder; and we will worship and return to you.' And Abraham took the wood of the burnt offering and laid it on Isaac his son, and he took in his hand the fire and the knife. So the two of them walked on together. And Isaac spoke to Abraham his father and said, 'My father!' And he said, 'Here I am, my son.' And he said, 'Behold, the fire and the wood, but where is the lamb for the burnt offering?' And Abraham said, 'God will provide for Himself the lamb for the burnt offering, my son.' So the two of them walked on together. Then they came to the place of which God had told him; and Abraham built the altar there, and arranged the wood, and bound his son

53

Isaac, and laid him on the altar on top of the wood. And Abraham stretched out his hand, and took the knife to slay his son. But the angel of the Lord called to him from heaven, and said, 'Abraham, Abraham!' And he said, 'Here I am.' And he said, 'Do not stretch out your hand against the lad, and do nothing to him; for now I know that you fear God, since you have not withheld your son, your only son, from Me.' Then Abraham raised his eyes and looked, and behold, behind him a ram caught in the thicket by his horns; and Abraham went and took the ram, and offered him up for a burnt offering in the place of his son. And Abraham called the name of that place The Lord Will Provide, as it is said to this day, 'In the mount of the Lord it will be provided.' Then the angel of the Lord called to Abraham a second time from heaven, and said, 'By Myself I have sworn, declares the Lord, because you have done this thing, and have not withheld your son, your only son, indeed I will greatly bless you, and I will greatly multiply your seed as the stars of the heavens, and as the sand which is on the seashore; and your seed shall possess the gate of their enemies. And in your seed all the nations of the earth shall be blessed, because you have obeyed My voice' " (Gen. 22:1-18).

Immediate Obedience

In this account of Abraham and Isaac the word "obedience" stands out. Notice first that Abraham's obedience was immediate. Verse 3 of Genesis 22 says, "So Abraham rose early in the morning and saddled his donkey." God had called Abraham to sacrifice his son on a distant mountain. This man of God could have delayed in responding, but he didn't. He rose early in the morning. He responded to the voice of God without delay.

This teaches us a great lesson about our relationship with God. The man or woman who responds immediately to God's call receives great blessing. Often we do not want to listen to the Lord, and so we delay in obeying. The longer we delay, the longer we miss the blessing. Also the work and testimony of God may suffer.

I think of this particularly in connection with the great task of world evangelism. So much more could be done if men and women would obey God's directives related to proclaiming the gospel of the Lord Jesus Christ. If you haven't become part of the team carrying the truth of God to the ends of the earth, don't delay any longer. Find your place and serve enthusiastically now.

Trusting Obedience

Second, Abraham demonstrated a very trusting obedience. When Abraham went on alone with his son, he said to his servants, "Stay here with the donkey, and I and the lad will go yonder; and we will worship and return to you" (Gen. 22:5). Notice that he used the plural—he *and* Isaac would come back together. He believed that God would keep His promises concerning Isaac. He knew that if he actually carried through with the sacrifice of Isaac that God could raise Isaac from the dead (see Heb. 11:17-19). That was trusting obedience.

We, too, can follow the plan of God confidently. Even when we cannot see the end of things, we can obey the Lord happily. We believe that God will carry out what He has promised to do. That is trusting obedience.

Complete Obedience

Third, Abraham obeyed completely. He was willing even to sacrifice his son at God's command. The Bible says, "And Abraham stretched out his hand, and took the knife to slay his son" (Gen. 22:10). What a scene that must have been. Abraham's heart must have been breaking as he proceeded to carry out God's order. I'm confident that confusion filled Abraham's heart as he prepared to sacrifice his son. But he obeyed nevertheless. He was ready to go all the way with God. That kind of obedience honors God.

We often miss the greatest blessings of life because we hold back, because we don't obey God totally. We don't allow God to have His way in certain areas of our lives. Someone has said, "Delay is the deadliest form of denial." Some of us have denied what God wants simply by delaying our obedience. That is defective obedience. It's much better to obey God's orders without reserve. This is especially true concerning the matter of world evangelism. The Lord looks for our total and complete response to His command.

Rewarded Obedience

Fourth, Abraham's obedience was rewarded. Listen to the promise of God: "Indeed I will greatly bless you, and I will greatly multiply your seed as the stars of the heavens, and as the sand which is

56

on the seashore; and your seed shall possess the gate of their enemies. And in your seed all the nations of the earth shall be blessed, because you have obeyed My voice" (Gen. 22:17,18).

Two great promises were given to Abraham as a result of his obedience—that God would bless him and that in Abraham many people would be blessed. No one could desire anything better than to have God's favor and provision and to be useful in the lives of others. It is no wonder that when Abraham came to the end of his life, he "breathed his last and died in a ripe old age, an old man and satisfied with life; and he was gathered to his people" (25:8).

When we enjoy the favor of God, then life has its greatest fulfillment. By listening to and obeying the voice of the Lord, we obtain a reward.

A Greater Obedience

Fifth, Abraham's obedience was the type of something far greater. In Hebrews 11 we read this commentary on this event in the life of Abraham: "By faith Abraham, when he was tested, offered up Isaac; and he who had received the promises was offering up his only begotten son; it was he to whom it was said, 'In Isaac your descendants shall be called.' He considered that God is able to raise men even from the dead; from which he also received him back as a type" (vv. 17-19).

Abraham's willingness to sacrifice Isaac pointed forward to God's giving His Son to die on our behalf. After Christ died, He rose from the dead, and He lives today. In Abraham's commitment of giving his son and then receiving him back again, we see Jesus' death and resurrection symbolized in a beautiful way.

Abraham has given us an inspiring example of the obedience of faith. When we follow his example, God will perfect His work in us. We will be privileged to give His message to others. Through the obedience of faith we present our lives and resources to God so that the gospel of Jesus Christ might go to the ends of the earth.

Chapter 13

The Death of Sarah

"Now Sarah lived one hundred and twenty-seven years; these were the years of the life of Sarah. And Sarah died in Kiriath-arba (that is, Hebron) in the land of Canaan; and Abraham went in to mourn for Sarah and to weep for her. Then Abraham rose from before his dead, and spoke to the sons of Heth, saying, 'I am a stranger and a sojourner among you; give me a burial site among you, that I may bury my dead out of my sight.' And the sons of Heth answered Abraham, saying to him, 'Hear us, my lord, you are a mighty prince among us; bury your dead in the choicest of our graves; none of us will refuse you his grave for burying your dead.' So Abraham rose and bowed to the people of the land, the sons of Heth. And he spoke with them, saying, 'If it is your wish for me to bury my dead out of my sight, hear me, and approach Ephron the son of Zohar for me, that he may give me the cave of Machpelah which he owns, which is at the end of his field; for the full price let him give it to me in your presence for a burial site.' Now Ephron was sitting among the sons of Heth; and Ephron the Hittite answered Abraham in the hearing of the sons of Heth; even of all who went in at the gate of his city, saying, 'No, my lord, hear me; I give you the field, and I give you the cave that is in it. In the presence of the sons of my people I give it to you; bury your dead.'

And Abraham bowed before the people of the land. And he spoke to Ephron in the hearing of the people of the land, saying, 'If you will only please listen to me; I will give the price of the field, accept it from me, that I may bury my dead there.' Then Ephron answered Abraham, saying to him, 'My lord, listen to me; a piece of land worth four hundred shekels of silver, what is that between me and you? So bury your dead.' And Abraham listened to Ephron; and Abraham weighed out for Ephron the silver which he had named in the hearing of the sons of Heth, four hundred shekels of silver, commercial standard. So Ephron's field, which was in Machpelah, which faced Mamre, the field and cave which was in it, and all the trees which were in the field, that were within all the confines of its border, were deeded over to Abraham for a possession in the presence of the sons of Heth, before all who went in at the gate of his city. And after this, Abraham buried Sarah his wife in the cave of the field at Machpelah facing Mamre (that is, Hebron) in the land of Canaan. So the field, and the cave that is in it, were deeded over to Abraham for a burial site by the sons of Heth" (Gen. 23:1-20).

Death—Common to All People

We have followed the lives of Abraham and Sarah through a number of chapters in Genesis. We have seen them as a couple chosen by God to be the beginning of a line that would culminate in the birth of Christ, the Saviour of men. We have watched them under various circumstances and have caught something of the love that Abraham had for Sarah and that Sarah had for her husband. Now we are suddenly brought face to face with the fact of death. At the age of 127 Sarah died.

Look at the scene. Abraham—a mighty man, a great prince, respected and loved—could not stay the hand of death. At that point he stood just as any other man on the face of the earth. Abraham came to mourn for Sarah. She whose beauty had captivated two kings now had to be buried out of sight.

The scene is very common. It touches our hearts. Abraham was bowed down with grief. Sarah was no longer with him. This lesson tells us again that we must all pass through this experience. Someone reading this right now might be suffering such a loss at this moment. Perhaps a person very dear to you has just passed away. It seems as if the best of life has been taken away from you. Look to the Lord from whom your help can come. In such a situation it is very good to know the Lord Jesus Christ and to have hope in Him.

While reflecting on this, let's remember that many men and women around the world do not have an answer in the hour of death. They do not have hope, because they have never heard the message of the Lord Jesus. When death comes with all of its terror and fear, they have no place to go. That lays upon all of us the privilege and responsibility of taking them the message of hope.

Abraham's Expectation of Life

It's significant to notice that Abraham did not return to his own land to bury Sarah. By faith he purchased a piece of ground in the land where God said his seed, or descendants, would live. This constitutes another step of faith on the part of faithful Abraham. His first tangible step in accepting God's promise of the land of Canaan came through the purchase of a burial place for his wife.

For the child of God, death, though hard and difficult, actually becomes the step by which we enter more fully into the promises of God. It's often been said that no one is really prepared to live until he is prepared to die. For the Christian, death means entrance into eternal life.

Many passages of Scripture speak about this wonderful fact. I love the testimony of the Apostle Paul: "We are of good courage, I say, and prefer rather to be absent from the body and to be at home with the Lord" (II Cor. 5:8). Also, "For to me, to live is Christ, and to die is gain" (Phil. 1:21). That is a note of victory and power through faith. That's why Abraham's significant step of faith came at the hour of death. In the midst of death he had hope in God.

Death doesn't end all. For the Christian, death is merely the beginning which ushers in eternal life. We should be enthusiastic about the fact that we have the message of life for a dying world. The world faces the crisis of death. It's especially important that we carry the message of life to those who have never heard it. They sit in darkness and under the shadow of death. But they can hear and know the truth of God. Then they, too, will be able to say, "For to me, to live is Christ, and to die is gain" (v. 21).

Chapter 14

A Wife for Isaac

"Now Abraham was old, advanced in age; and the Lord had blessed Abraham in every way. And Abraham said to his servant, the oldest of his household, who had charge of all that he owned, 'Please place your hand under my thigh, and I will make you swear by the Lord, the God of heaven and the God of earth, that you shall not take a wife for my son from the daughters of the Canaanites, among whom I live, but you shall go to my country and to my relatives, and take a wife for my son Isaac.' And the servant said to him, 'Suppose the woman will not be willing to follow me to this land; should I take your son back to the land from where you came?' Then Abraham said to him, 'Beware lest you take my son back there! The Lord, the God of heaven, who took me from my father's house and from the land of my birth, and who spoke to me, and who swore to me, saying, "To your descendants I will give this land", He will send His angel before you, and you will take a wife for my son from there. But if the woman is not willing to follow you, then you will be free from this my oath; only do not take my son back there.' So the servant placed his hand under the thigh of Abraham his master, and swore to him concerning this matter. Then the servant took ten camels from the camels of his master, and set out with a variety of good things of his master's in his hand; and he arose,

and went to Mesopotamia, to the city of Nahor.
And he made the camels kneel down outside the
city by the well of water at evening time, the time
when women go out to draw water. And he said, 'O
Lord, the God of my master Abraham, please
grant me success today, and show lovingkindness
to my master Abraham'' (Gen. 24:1-12).

Abraham's Instructions to His Servant

We are looking at one of the most beautiful and
significant passages of the Old Testament—the
obtaining of a wife for Isaac, the son of promise.
His wife would share in those promises and play a
large part in them.

This passage of Scripture presents the fact that
Abraham gave two important instructions to his
trusted servant. First, the wife for Isaac should not
be chosen from among the daughters of the Canaanites. Abraham did not give this directive because
he felt himself and his family to be superior to the
Canaanites. Neither did he make that request
because he feared the Canaanites would oppose
such a marriage. Quite a few of their daughters
would undoubtedly have considered it an honor to
become the wife of Abraham's son. The reason for
Abraham's instruction is summed up in the question, "Can two walk together, except they be
agreed?" (Amos 3:3, KJV). Isaac was a child of
God, a believer. The people of Canaan did not
believe in Abraham's God. Therefore, they did not
have the most important thing in common—faith
in the Lord.

The principle that Abraham stood for still ap-
plies today. A follower of Jesus Christ should con-

sider marriage only with someone of like precious faith. It is contrary to the will of God for a child of light to take up an intimate lifetime association with one who has not received the light of the gospel. Many people have come to grief because they have ignored this. If you are contemplating marriage, let me urge you to be sure that your partner is also a follower of the Lord Jesus Christ.

Second, Abraham made it plain that Isaac should not leave Canaan to get a wife. The wife would have to come to Canaan, the land of promise that God had given to them. Was this stubbornness on the part of Abraham? By no means. God had led him to Canaan. In such an important matter as marriage, this directive of the Lord should be remembered. Isaac should not leave Canaan, even for the sake of marriage. It was God's plan for Isaac to continue in Canaan.

This teaches us a second essential for a successful marriage. It should be arranged in line with God's will as He reveals that will to us. It is not to be a casual happenstance.

Followers of the Lord have often had to take a stand on this issue. They knew the path along which God was leading them. They also knew that if they should marry person A or B or C, then that marriage relationship would take them away from the clear plan of God.

So two great principles are made clear in this passage. First, in marriage the follower of the Lord Jesus Christ should join only with another believer. Second, such a marriage should be in harmony with God's plan for the lives of both individuals.

Servant's Petition for Guidance

Isn't it interesting that Abraham's trusted servant began his search by asking the Lord for guidance? He knew that he could not rely on his own judgment alone. He needed divine direction. The important choice of a life partner should be bathed in prayer, and an appeal should be made for God to make His will plain.

Listen to what the servant said: "O Lord, the God of my master Abraham, please grant me success today, and show lovingkindness to my master Abraham" (Gen. 24:12). In the great choices of life—in fact, in all choices—we should be concerned about following God's direction.

God's Answer

The remaining verses in Genesis 24 show us that God answered. Abraham's servant was directed to the right person (see vv. 13-27). Rebekah accepted the invitation to become the wife of Isaac (see vv. 48-59), and they lived happily after that. God will also direct us as we seek His will.

A Type of Jesus Christ and His Bride

As we study this account of the choice of a wife for Isaac, we realize that it pictures the Lord Jesus Christ, the Bridegroom, and His Bride, the Church. The Lord Jesus is seeking to complete His Bride. Many precious people must still be brought to faith in the Lord Jesus. You and I have the opportunity of seeking them as the trusted servant of Abraham sought a bride for Isaac. We go out in Jesus' name to win others for our Master.

The Lord Jesus is calling us to carry the gospel message far and wide. Let's be sure that we are actively participating in the big job of world evangelism. That means praying and giving and asking the Lord just what He wants our part to be on the team that is doing His work.

The servant of Abraham said, "I being in the way, the Lord led me" (Gen. 24:27, KJV). We can have God's guidance as we carry out God's work. It will be a great day when the Lord Jesus comes again. Then He will receive His Bride, the Church, who will be without "spot or wrinkle or any such thing" (Eph. 5:27).

Chapter 15

Esau—The Profane Person

"And Isaac prayed to the Lord on behalf of his wife, because she was barren; and the Lord answered him and Rebekah his wife conceived. But the children struggled together within her; and she said, 'If it is so, why then am I this way?' So she went to inquire of the Lord. And the Lord said to her, 'Two nations are in your womb; and two peoples shall be separated from your body; and one people shall be stronger than the other; and the older shall serve the younger.' When her days to be delivered were fulfilled, behold, there were twins in her womb. Now the first came forth red, all over like a hairy garment; and they named him Esau. And afterward his brother came forth with his hand holding on to Esau's heel, so his name was called Jacob; and Isaac was sixty years old when she gave birth to them. When the boys grew up, Esau became a skillful hunter, a man of the field; but Jacob was a peaceful man, living in tents. Now Isaac loved Esau, because he had a taste for game; but Rebekah loved Jacob. And when Jacob had cooked stew, Esau came in from the field and he was famished; and Esau said to Jacob, 'Please let me have a swallow of that red stuff there, for I am famished.' Therefore his name was called Edom. But Jacob said, 'First sell me your birthright.' And Esau said, 'Behold, I am about to die; so of what use then is the birthright to me?' And Jacob said, 'First swear to me'; so he swore to him, and sold his birthright to Jacob. Then Jacob gave Esau bread and lentil stew; and he ate and drank, and rose and went on his way. Thus Esau despised his birthright" (Gen. 25:21-34).

There are many interesting commentaries in the Bible about various Scripture passages. We find such a commentary in Hebrews 12:16 which refers to Esau. There the Bible says, "That there be no immoral or godless person like Esau, who sold his own birthright for a single meal."

In sacred history we read of many individuals who made a terrible mess of their lives. Think of Cain, the first murderer in the Bible. He had the same opportunities as Abel; yet Cain was very stubborn and chose his own way to worship God.

Think of King Saul, who had many opportunities to lead the people of God in a right way. But he did not give God first place, and Saul came to a very miserable end.

What shall we say of Absalom, the son of David, who tried to steal the hearts of the nation? He was not faithful to God or to his father. He ended up hanging by his head from a tree.

Think of Judas, one of the Twelve. He had heard the enlightened teachings of Jesus. He had enjoyed the Lord's fellowship. Yet Judas betrayed his Master. Of him the Lord said, "It would have been good for that man if he had not been born" (Matt. 26:24).

Selling His Birthright

Esau's story is one of the saddest in the Bible. In one sense he was a very attractive person. No doubt he was a man of great physical strength. He excelled as a hunter. If he had lived in modern times, he probably would have been a star athlete. Many people must have said about Esau, "There goes a real man."

But his story has another side. All of his life revolved around material rather than spiritual things. Consequently, Genesis 25 tells how Esau despised his birthright and sold it to Jacob. The birthright belonged as a special privilege to the firstborn in a family. Among the Israelites it meant not only receiving the larger part of the inheritance, but it also included a very special spiritual blessing. But because Esau had an eye only for material things, he despised his birthright. The birthright was just too intangible and too far in the future for him.

The Bible recounts that Esau returned from the hunt tired and hungry (v. 29). He asked for the food which Jacob had prepared. Jacob immediately said, "Sell me your birthright" (v. 31). Esau said, in effect, "I'm ready to die right now for lack of food. My birthright won't do me any good. You can have it" (v. 32). In other words, Esau was actually saying, "I can see, feel and taste a meal. That means more to me than a birthright. Why should I worry about the future? I can have the meal in my hands right *now*. That's more important than my birthright."

The Bible calls Esau a profane, or godless, person (Heb. 12:16, KJV). He was one of the first materialists. He had the philosophy, "Eat, drink and be merry, for tomorrow we die." The things of God meant little to him; he was interested only in the things he could see and touch.

Many Modern Esaus

There are many modern Esaus. The passing things of this world have more importance for them than the things of God. Several years ago we had the opportunity of seeing again a young man whom we had known when he was small. He was a missionary kid. We had watched him grow up. He had had tremendous opportunities to be acquainted with spiritual things. But by a series of poor decisions and wrong steps, this young man got into the field of recording very worldly music with immoral words. We talked with him at length when we saw him again. We said, "Do you recognize that the words of the songs you are recording have a very bad meaning?" He answered that he realized that. We then asked him, "Does it bother you that you are responsible for recording that music?" He said, "Yes, at times it does bother me." We said, "What do you do about it?" "Well," he said, "the money I earn speaks so loudly that, even though my conscience objects at times, it is drowned out by the stronger voice of the comfortable life I live and everything I have at my disposal." That young man is a modern Esau.

I think also of a young man in Ecuador. He at first seemed ready to accept the Lord as his Saviour. Then he drew back and completely lost interest in attending the Bible meetings. When asked why, he said, "Do you think I want to lose my inheritance?" His family had warned him that if he followed the way of the gospel, they would disinherit him. He chose his earthly inheritance instead of God.

Many people are walking far from God, not

because they are aggressively rejecting Him but because they are so interested in the things of the world that they have no time to think about their Creator. It's tragic when a person spends his life worshiping material things, because when life ends, the material things have to be left behind.

Let's invest our lives in what really counts for time and for eternity. We should spend our lives helping others as a result of committing ourselves to God. Jim Elliot was right when he said, "He is no fool who gives what he cannot keep to gain what he cannot lose."

Blessed is the man or woman who puts God first, who has his or her priorities straight and who lives for the purpose God intends. What is God's purpose for us? It is first that we shall know Him, then that by His grace we shall become like Him and finally that we shall be used to bless others. Primarily that means we should be part of that group of men and women who are determined to carry the gospel of Jesus Christ to those who have not heard it.